HISTORYTIME

W0317751

The Bridge of Swords

Cornelsen

History Time
The Bridge of Swords

Erarbeitet von
Doris Ertel-Zellner und Reinhold Zellner, München

Zeichnungen
Bernd Kissel, Überherrn-Berus

Verlagsredaktion
Michael Dunkel • Jennifer O'Hagan (Assistenz)

Umschlaggestaltung
HOX designgroup – Kay Bach, Köln

Layout und technische Umsetzung
Buch und Gestaltung – Britta Dieterle, Berlin

Bildquellen
Alamy, Abingdon (S. 23 oben: Roy Rainford/Robert Harding Picture Library Ltd, unten: Photo 12/Hachedé); Corbis, Düsseldorf (S. 22 unten: Jonathan Hession/Touchstone/Bureau L.A. Collection)

www.cornelsen.de

1. Auflage, 5. Druck 2021

Alle Drucke dieser Ausgabe sind inhaltlich unverändert
und können im Unterricht nebeneinander verwendet werden.

Druck: Esser printSolutions GmbH, Bretten

ISBN: 978-3-06-033223-6

PEFC
PEFC/04-31-2851

PEFC zertifiziert
Dieses Produkt stammt aus nachhaltig bewirtschafteten Wäldern und kontrollierten Quellen.

www.pefc.de

East Street
That's all our money!
BOOKIE
Give me that money! I have a great idea!
!?
Follow me!
BOOKIE
Don't tell me you want to bet all our money on Hamlet!
HAMLET IS IN THE LEAD ...
... WITH JABBERWOCKY CLOSE BEHIND!
HAMLET HESITATES! AND NOW JABBERWOCKY ATTACKS! HE PASSES HAMLET!
!?
4
6
3
And just what can we tell Grandma now? You know what she's going to say!?
"Your father gambled away a lot of money when he was young ... And before him your grandfather and your great-grandfather, and before **him** ..."

Camelot in the year 475
You've lost everything!
You owe us a favour!
Close by
To the glory of our great king, King Arthur!

Now tell me about your adventures!
I defeated the Beast of the Bottomless Lake!
And I freed the King of Gwynedd's beautiful daughter from her curse!
To your health, Sir Tristan and Sir Gawain!
One of our circle has left us forever!
But let us celebrate the deeds of the other two, Sir Perceval and Sir Lancelot!
I won the tournament for Queen Guinevere!
And I almost discovered the Holy Grail for the third time!
The deeds of King Arthur's Round Table will be celebrated for thousands of years!

Now don't tell me you had another of your premonitions again, Merlin!
Merlin's premonitions always come true.
?!
Queen Guinevere ...
... after leaving her father's castle ...
... on her way home ...
... the Red Knight abducted her!!!

My wife!
In the hands of that villain!
No one has ever been able to get into his castle!
Then I will be the first!
I will free the queen!
The Red Knight is a powerful enemy.
But you are not alone!
Are you in despair? I will be there. Just follow the sign!
Later
I'm looking forward to tomorrow's tour-nament!
Everyone will envy us because we're Lancelot's squires!
Even a knight like Lancelot will not survive a battle against the Red Knight!
!?
It will surely be his end!
A battle with the Red Knight!
That will surely be our end, too!
I don't want to die!

And you won't, either!
A bet is a bet!
?
This will be the biggest adventure of your lives!
?!
Why are you wearing those silly outfits?
?!
Don't worry, Grandma!
You're going to be proud of us!
God be with you, noble knight!

Later
Something about my squires seems strange to me today ...
So what!? I must rescue Guinevere!
!?
Personally, I don't think you will!
Personally, I REALLY don't think you will!
And I would say you don't have a chance at all!
A Knight of the Round Table does not fear a ...
Are you sure?

Not really!
I love knights in armour! They're so crunchy!
And which one of us gets the best bit?
Hee hee hee!
You there in the middle, of course!
Even a child could see you're the leader.
What can a child see?
That I'm the leader. It's crystal clear, isn't it?!
Huh?

I'm the leader! I'm the leader!
He's crazy!
You saved my life. I'll never forget that!
And now what?
An hour later
The Forest of Fear.
We have to go through there!?
But how?

I have no idea at all!
!
Hamlet, come back!
Woof!
Ouch!
Woof!
!?
!?
Choke!
SMACK
SKRET
Over here!
We have to help him!
Will you please close your mouth when you're chewing!
Let's get out of here!
SKRT

And who are YOU?
Pant.
Beyond this wood lies the fortress of the Red Knight.
And I'm his caretaker.
Spirits, be on your way! Leave this earthly world, I say! Leave at once, return to hell. Let peace reign, and all be well.
KA-ZING
The spirits of darkness should have swallowed YOU.
But I keep mixing up these Latin spells!
SCRATCH! SCRATCH!
If it wasn't for you, noble knight, my own spells would have destroyed me! From this day on, YOU are my master!
!?
Well, actually, he's the one who saved you!

The hardest test still lies before you!

The Bridge of Swords!
It's very dangerous!
But it's a question of honour or disgrace.

*Shakespeare, Hamlet, Act 3

SCREACH
Guinevere! I'm coming!
Enter. I've been expecting you!

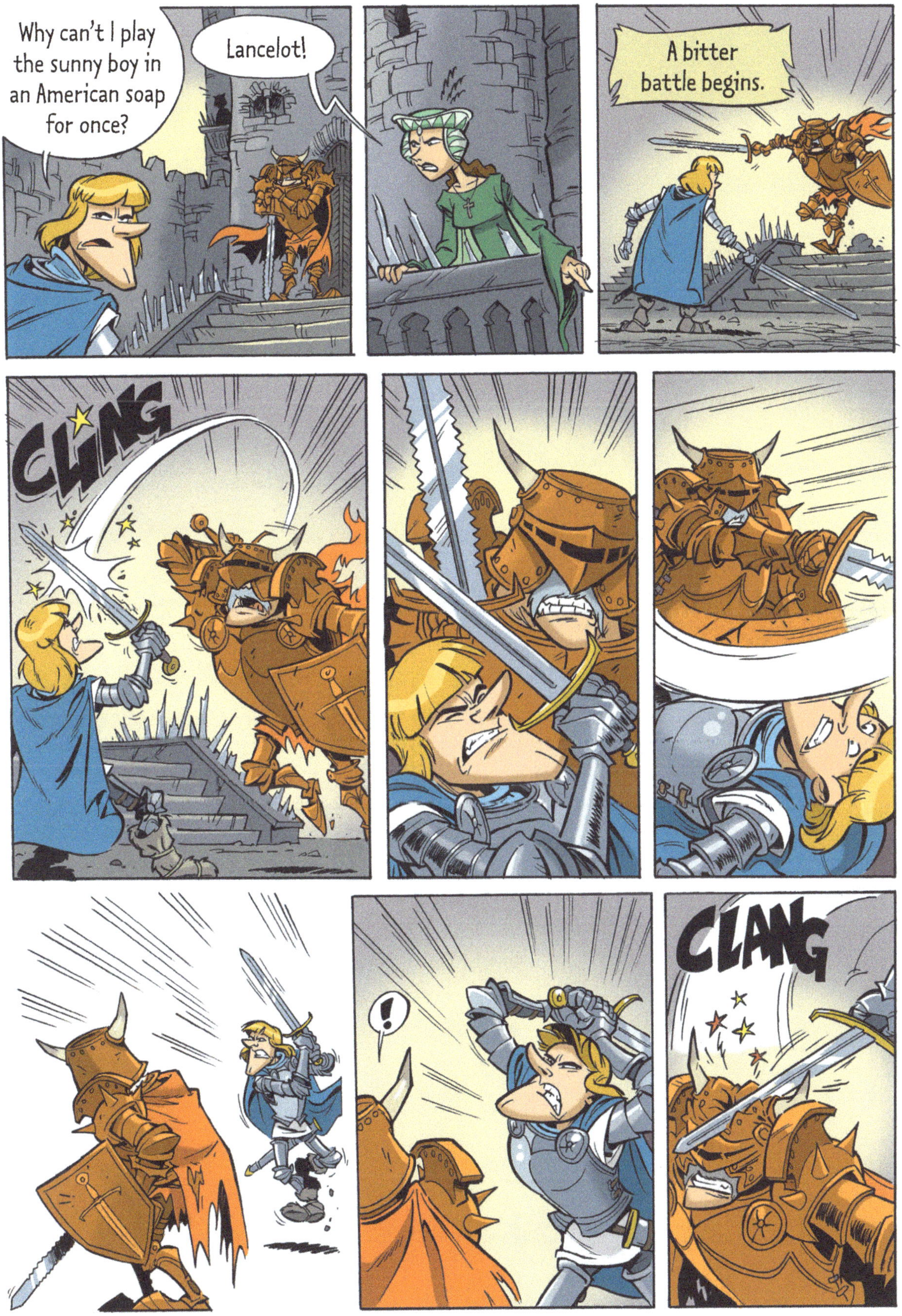
Why can't I play the sunny boy in an American soap for once?
Lancelot!
A bitter battle begins.
CLING
!
CLANG

Promise your loyalty to King Arthur and I'll let you live!
Help me up!
It's not a disgrace to surrender to the mighty Sir Lancelot.
Fair Queen, I'm here to rescue you!
He doesn't realize yet what he's in for!
Do you know how late you are?
You're the lamest knight who has ever come to my rescue!
?!

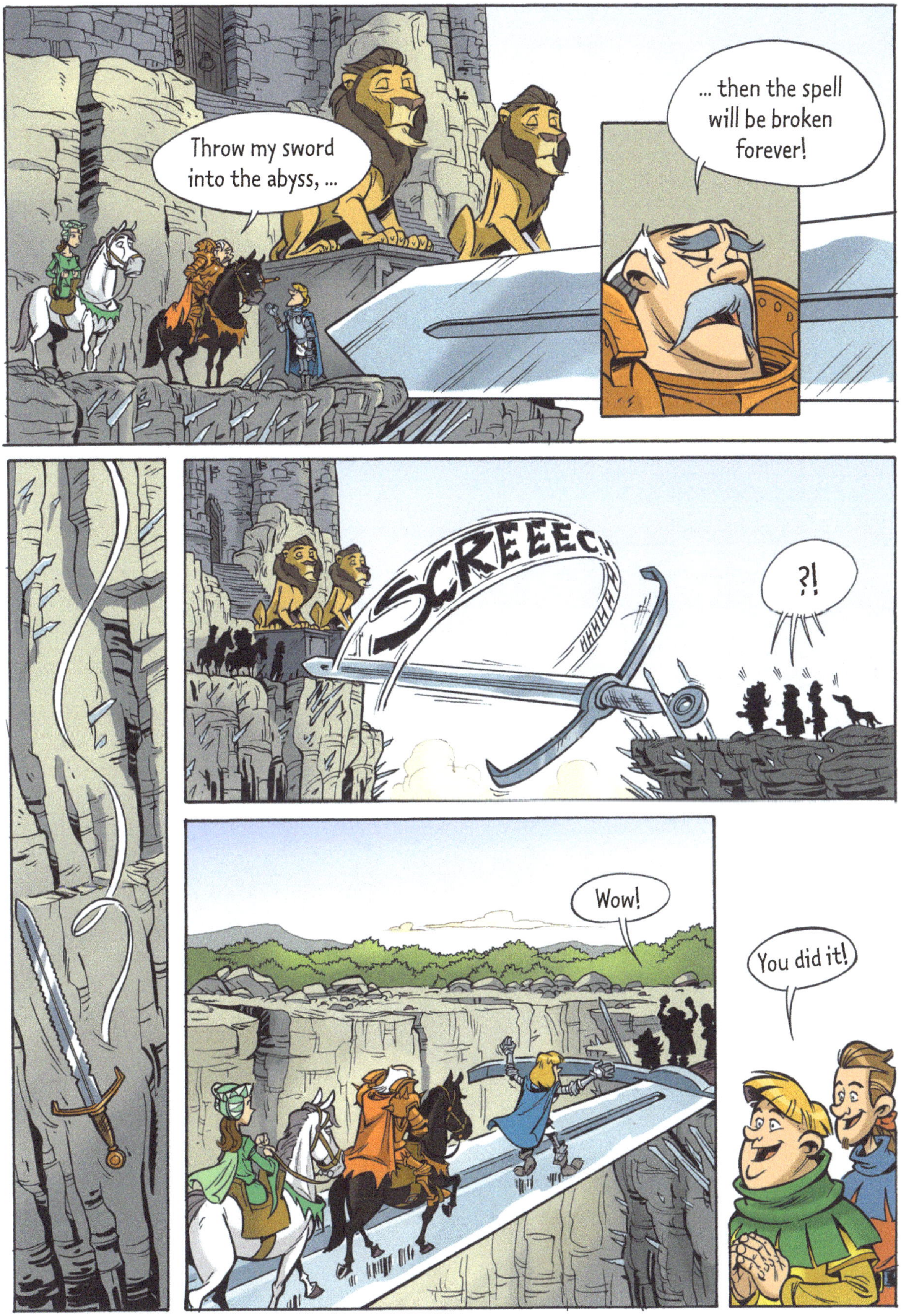

Throw my sword into the abyss, ...
... then the spell will be broken forever!
SCREEECH
?!
Wow!
You did it!

Later
I thank you for your loyal service. From this day on, you are your own master!
That's good timing! A position just opened up ...
Medieval Times
Snow White with cottage in the wood seeks seventh dwarf - must be strong and good
And their journey back was peaceful and calm.
Who's the leader here?
Upon their return they received a spectacular reception.
Long live the Queen!
Lancelot, our hero!

Bravo!
CLAP CLAP
The evil spell is broken.
We've been reunited after such a long time.
Long live the Round Table!
All's well that ends well!

History file: King Arthur

Grandma, there are so many books and films about King Arthur – was he a real person or is he just the hero of a legend?

Some historians[1] think that King Arthur was a real person in the late 5th and early 6th centuries[2], others think he wasn't a real person at all. However, he became famous with a book from the 12th century – it's the *History of the Kings of Britain* by Geoffrey of Monmouth. More and more poems and stories appeared[3] in England and later in France and Germany about the great hero who successfully defended[4] his country against the Saxons and set up a large kingdom[5]. King Arthur, the Knights of the Round Table and Merlin, the wise wizard[6], keep our imagination alive[7] even today.

How did Arthur become king?

There was a time when Britain had no king or queen, and a prophecy[8] said that only the boy or man who could easily pull out a sword from a very big stone could become king. Many people tried, but only young Arthur was successful[9]. He pulled out the sword and he became the new king.

Was this sword the magic sword Excalibur?

Yes, it was. But other stories tell a different version: Arthur got Excalibur from the mysterious Lady of the Lake, a nymph who stretched her arm out[10] from her lake to give the magic sword to Arthur, and one day the sword should also be returned to the lake.

What do you know about Camelot?

Camelot was a castle. Arthur built it after he became king. It was the place where King Arthur and the Knights of the Round Table gathered[11]. The knights started their journeys at Camelot. They went to fight the powers of darkness[12]. When they returned to the castle they told the stories of their deeds, and so the Round Table became more and more famous.

This scene from the film *King Arthur* (2004) shows Lancelot (left), Guinevere (centre) and Arthur (right): the film is another interpretation of the legend of King Arthur and the Knights of the Round Table which dates back to the 12th century.

But why was it a round table?

Nobody could sit at the head[13] of a round table – none of the knights, and not even the king – and so they were all equal[14].

What do we know about the Knights of the Round Table?

The knights were very brave[15] men. Their most important qualities[16] were the love of God and men, honour, dignity[17], loyalty to the king and courage[18]. The knights went to war[19] for their king, they defeated the most dangerous enemies and fought against supernatural powers[20], but they also had to help the poor and protect the ladies, or, as they were often called at the time, damsels. The most famous knights are Sir Gawain, Sir Galahad, Sir Tristan, Sir Percival and Sir Lancelot.
Sir Lancelot was the greatest warrior[21] of them all, but he also had a big problem: he fell desperately in love with King Arthur's wife Guinevere – and she fell in love with him.

When people talk about King Arthur and the Knights of the Round Table, they often talk about the quest for the Holy Grail[22]. What is this Holy Grail?

This illustration from the 15th century shows the Holy Grail and the Knights of the Round Table.

The ruins of Tintagel Castle in Cornwall: some people think it was one of Arthur's castles.

It's not clear what the Holy Grail really is – some sources[23] say it's a cup, others say it's a plate[24] or even a stone, but all agree it's something very valuable[25]. One famous story about the Holy Grail says it was the cup from the Last Supper[26] which held the blood[27] of Jesus Christ. However, this cup was lost at one point, and the greatest and most honourable[28] task for King Arthur's knights was to search[29] for it and find it.

1 **historian** | Historiker(in) ▪ 2 **century** | Jahrhundert ▪ 3 (to) **appear** | veröffentlicht werden ▪ 4 (to) **defend** | verteidigen ▪ 5 **kingdom** | Königreich ▪ 6 **wizard** | Zauberer ▪ 7 (to) **keep the imagination alive** | die Fantasie wachhalten ▪ 8 **prophecy** | Weissagung ▪ 9 **successful** | erfolgreich ▪ 10 (to) **stretch an arm out** | einen Arm (her)ausstrecken ▪ 11 (to) **gather** | sich versammeln ▪ 12 **the powers of darkness** | die Mächte der Finsternis ▪ 13 **head** | Kopf ▪ 14 **equal** | gleichberechtigt ▪ 15 **brave** | mutig ▪ 16 **quality** | Wert; Eigenschaft ▪ 17 **dignity** | Würde ▪ 18 **courage** | Mut ▪ 19 **war** | Krieg ▪ 20 **supernatural powers** | übernatürliche Kräfte ▪ 21 **warrior** | Krieger(in) ▪ 22 **the quest for the Holy Grail** | die Suche nach dem Heiligen Gral ▪ 23 **source** | Quelle ▪ 24 **plate** | Teller ▪ 25 **valuable** | wertvoll ▪ 26 **the Last Supper** | das Letzte Abendmahl ▪ 27 **blood** | Blut ▪ 28 **honourable** | ehrenhaft ▪ 29 (to) **search** | suchen

Vocabulary

(to) **abduct** [æb'dʌkt] entführen
  they let themselves get abducted sie lassen sich entführen
able ['eɪbl]: (to) **be able to do something** etwas tun können
abyss [ə'bɪs] Abgrund
almost ['ɔ:lməʊst] fast
armour ['ɑ:mə] (Ritter)rüstung
(to) **attack** [ə'tæk] angreifen

battle ['bætl] Kampf
bet [bet] Wette
beyond [bɪ'jɒnd] jenseits
boar [bɔ:] Eber *(Wildschwein)*
  boar hide Fell/Haut eines Ebers

calm [kɑ:m] ruhig
caretaker ['keəteɪkə] (Guts)verwalter(in)
(to) **chew** [tʃu:] kauen
close [kləʊs] knapp
  close by (ganz) in der Nähe
crazy ['kreɪzi] verrückt
crunchy ['krʌntʃi] knusprig, knackig
crystal clear [ˌkrɪstl'klɪə] glasklar
curse [kɜ:s] Fluch
  cursed verhext; mit einem Fluch belegt

darkness ['dɑ:knəs] Dunkelheit
deed [di:d] Tat
(to) **defeat** [dɪ'fi:t] besiegen
despair [dɪ'speə]: (to) **be in despair** verzweifelt sein
(to) **discover** [dɪ'skʌvə] entdecken
disgrace [dɪs'greɪs] Schande
dwarf [dwɔ:f] Zwerg

earthly ['ɜ:θli] irdisch
either ['aɪðə] auch nicht
enemy ['enəmi] Feind(in)
(to) **envy** ['envi] beneiden
ever ['evə] jemals
evil ['i:vl] böse
(to) **expect** [ɪk'spekt] erwarten

fair [feə] *hier:* liebreizend
(to) **fear** [fɪə] fürchten

forest ['fɒrɪst] Wald
  Forest of Fear Wald des Schreckens
forever [fər'evə] für immer
fortress ['fɔ:trəs] Festung
(to) **free** [fri:] befreien

(to) **gamble** ['gæmbl]: (to) **gamble away** verspielen
(to) **get out** [ˌget'aʊt]: **Let's get out of here!** Lass uns hier verschwinden!
glory ['glɔ:ri] Ruhm
God [gɒd]: **God be with you!** Gott sei mit dir/Ihnen/euch!
grandma ['grænmɑ:] Oma
great-grandfather [ˌgreɪt'grænfɑ:ðə] Urgroßvater

health [helθ]: **To your health!** Auf dein/Ihr/euer Wohl!
hell [hel] Hölle
hero ['hɪərəʊ] Held
(to) **hesitate** ['hezɪteɪt] zögern
honour ['ɒnə] Ehre

(to) **keep** [ki:p]: (to) **keep mixing up something** etwas ständing verwechseln
king [kɪŋ] König
knight [naɪt] Ritter
  Knight of the Round Table Ritter der Tafelrunde

lame [leɪm] lahm
lead [li:d]: (to) **be in the lead** in Führung liegen
(to) **lie** [laɪ] liegen
loyal ['lɔɪəl] treu
  loyal service treue Dienste
loyalty ['lɔɪəlti] Treue

master ['mɑ:stə] Herr
medieval [ˌmedi'i:vl] mittelalterlich
mighty ['maɪti] mächtig; stark

noble ['nəʊbl] edel; adlig

once [wʌns]: **at once** sofort
(to) **owe** [əʊ]: (to) **owe someone a favour** jemandem einen Gefallen schulden
own [əʊn] eigene(r, -s)

(to) **pass** [pɑ:s] überholen
peace [pi:s] Frieden
peaceful ['pi:sfl] friedlich
powerful ['paʊəfl] mächtig; stark
premonition [ˌpremə'nɪʃn] (böse) Vorahnung
(to) **promise** ['prɒmɪs] *hier:* schwören
(to) **protect** [prə'tekt] schützen

queen [kwi:n] Königin

(to) **realize** ['ri:əlaɪz] erkennen
(to) **receive** [rɪ'si:v]: (to) **receive a spectacular reception** spektakulär empfangen werden
(to) **reign** [reɪn] regieren
(to) **rescue** ['reskju:] retten
(to) **return** [rɪ'tɜ:n] zurückkehren
reunited [ˌri:ju'naɪtɪd] wiedervereint

(to) **seek** [si:k] suchen
(to) **seem** [si:m] scheinen
soap [səʊp] *hier:* Seifenoper
spell [spel] Zauberspruch
spirit ['spɪrɪt] Geist
squire ['skwaɪə] Knappe
supposed [sə'pəʊzd]: (to) **be supposed to do something** etwas tun sollen
(to) **surrender** [sə'rendə] sich ergeben
(to) **survive** [sə'vaɪv] überleben
(to) **swallow** ['swɒləʊ] verschlingen
sword [sɔ:d] Schwert

tournament ['tɔ:nəmənt] Turnier

villain ['vɪlən] Bösewicht; Schurke

wife [waɪf] (Ehe)frau
wood [wʊd] Wald
the worst [wɜ:st] das Schlimmste